A D V I C E

TO THE

O F F I C E R S

OF THE

B R I T I S H   A R M Y:

With the ADDITION of some Hints to the Drummer and Private Soldier.

RIDICULUM ACRI
FORTIUS ET MELIUS PLERUMQUE SECAT RES.

Safe from the Bar, the Pulpit and the Throne,
Yet touch'd and mov'd by Ridicule alone.

THE SIXTH EDITION.

L O N D O N:

Printed by W. RICHARDSON, for G. KEARSLEY in Fleet-street.
M DCC LXXXIII.

ENTERED AT STATIONERS HALL.

Reprinted 1992
by United States Historical
Research Service
Schenectady, New York
ISBN 0-9633659-0-8

THOUGH the very extensive and rapid sale of this little volume, together with the general approbation of the public, particularly of such gentlemen, as, from their professional character, we must allow to be the most competent judges, may be thought a sufficient testimony of its merit, yet as the judgment of the critics may serve the more strongly to ratify and confirm it, the publisher has taken upon himself to insert the following strictures, extracted from the different Reviews and Magazines.

Maty's *Review* for November 1782.

"This entertaining little piece of raillery, for which I have to return my thanks to the unknown author, yields to its model, Swift's Advice to Servants, in nothing but having come after it. In wit, satire, knowledge of the world, elegance of manners, and indignation at contemptible vice, it is equal, and in object it is much superior; for what is the endeavour to correct those who cannot read, whom we ourselves make what they are, and who, *cæteris paribus*, are as good as ourselves; what is this in comparison of the attempt to reform that body (or rather I should hope the few disgraceful individuals of that body) which ought to be every thing that is humane and generous, and upon whose conduct the national character depends, more than upon that of any other body of men whatever? The book will have this effect: for, as it is soon read, is pleasantly written, and abounds in hits which the most stupid corporal cannot miss, it will be in every regiment, ready to seize and fasten upon ridicule the instant it appears."

British *Magazine and Review* for December 1782.

"The sensible and ingenious author of this very interesting little work, hath, with peculiar spirit and exactness, marked out in a vein of irony the actual duty and rule of conduct for every officer in the
army,

army, from a commander in chief to a drum-major, omitting no single circumstance that it behoves each rank to be acquainted with; but we are deceived if he has not particular characters in view in some parts of his instructions, and in particular his address to commanders in chief.———

"But we will not anticipate the pleasure our sensible military readers will receive in perusing this pleasing pamphlet, which should be read at least once a week at every mess in Great Britain and its dependencies."

Critical Review for December 1782.

"This little tract is one of the severest satires which we remember to have seen; it is similar to Swift's Advice to Servants; and, by the ironical reason for each direction, conveys the keenest reproof for conduct which would disgrace the lowest followers of a regiment. We would recommend this agreeable monitor to the army in general; a good officer will be as little affected by these sarcasms as a respectable divine by Foote's Minor, or an intelligent physician by Garth's Dispensary. If there are any who, from youthful impetuosity, or a misplaced confidence in their own conduct and abilities, have realized this satire, we would advise them publicly to join in the laugh at the author's wit; and privately, by cool reflection, to discover their errors; and, by a serious and determined resolution, endeavour to amend them.

"The author has very politely concluded with the well-known adage, *qui capit, ille facit;* so that no one can pretend to be angry, who does not appear to feel the force of his ridicule, and to acknowledge its justice."

Gentleman's Magazine for January 1783.

"This little volume, which is by no mean hand, gives ironical advice to all ranks of officers, from the commander in chief down to the corporal and drum-major. It is evidently framed on the model of Swift's Advice to Servants, and exhibits a good copy of an excellent original.———

"The success that has attended this performance will probably produce an inundation of Advices; and Law, Physic, and Divinity, as well as the Navy, we doubt not, will have their Advisers. That they will be as well qualified as the present, can hardly be expected.

European

European Magazine for January 1783.

" This is one of the moſt laughable pieces of irony that has appeared ſince Swift provoked the riſible muſcles. We can trace many living charaċters in this animated performance, and, in bold colouring above the reſt, we readily diſcovered the lean and ſlipper'd Pantaloon of Mars.

London Magazine for February 1783.

" Let them behold (ſays the Roman ſatiriſt) the fair form of Virtue, that they may conſume with the anguiſh of repentant ſorrow for having forſook her." This writer, to effeċt the ſame good purpoſe, holds up the image of vice and folly in their native colours, and with an exaċt and undiſguiſed delineation of their lineaments, in order to ſhame men out of a diſgraceful and unworthy conneċtion with ſuch odious and ridiculous monſters. The deſign is truly laudable; and the execution is maſterly. The advice, though in form gay and ironical, yet in reality, is ſerious and pointed. No one who reads this exquiſite piece, if he hath the feelings of virtue, if he poſſeſſes the generous pride of patriotiſm, however he may be diverted by the writer's happy talent at ridicule, but muſt, at the concluſion, find his pleaſure repreſſed by mingled indignation and concern: and while he pathetically exclaims " Are theſe things ſo?"—He will only lament, but not wonder, that the ſun of Britain is ſhorn of his beams!"

Monthly Review for February 1783.

" This author diſcloſes a rich vein of wit. His advice, though clothed in the lighter form of irony, diſcovers a ſolid and penetrating judgment: and, while he holds a mirror up, that refleċts the true features of vice and folly, he attempts to make ingenuous ſhame accompliſh the work of rational conviċtion.

> Safe from the bar, the pulpit, and the throne,
> Yet touched and mov'd by ridicule alone.

For there are thoſe who may be laughed out of vice and folly, when all the powers of argument, and all the ſanċtions of religion, prove ineffeċtual to reclaim them.

"It appears to be the wish of this truly ingenious writer, to contribute his part towards restoring the credit of the army, by checking the still further progress of those abuses and irregularities that have of late so much sullied its honour, and diminished its importance, in the view of other countries, as well as in the estimation of the wiser part of our own; and by inspiring every officer with sentiments worthy the duty and character of British soldiers."

CONTENTS.

a 2   CHAP.

Just Published, *Price Two Shillings*,

THE ART OF PLEASING ; or, INSTRUCTIONS for YOUTH in the firſt Stage ot Life, in a Series of Letters to the PRESENT EARL OF CHESTERFIELD, by the late

PHILIP EARL OF CHESTERFIELD.

A Periodical Publication ſpeaks of this Work in the following Terms:

" This Collection confiſts of Fourteen Let-
" ters, written upon a variety of intereſting
" ſubjects ; they are all so truly important,
" and pleaſing likewiſe, that we know not
" which poſſeſſes the moſt merit. Every
" young man (of taſte and fortune parti-
" cularly) ought to read them with the
" greateſt attention."

" The late LORD CHESTERFIELD wrote .them
" from Bath to the preſent Lord, when he
" was under the tuition of the unfortunate
" Dr. Dodd."

" They are totally diſtinct from his *Letters* to
" his *Son*, publiſhed ſome years ſince."

INTRODUCTION.

IT may, perhaps, to many perfons appear quite needlefs to publifh any new fyftems of advice, after the infinite number that have already made their appearance in the world: for, befides thofe fo diftinguifhed in the title-page, all the treatifes on ethics, as well as the fermons of our divines, and the fyftems of œconomy and politenefs, may be ranked under that denomination. It is an old obfervation, that there are more ready to give, than to take, advice; and, in the fame manner, we may affert, without going far beyond the bounds of truth, that there

A   are

are at prefent, in the world, more authors than readers. The particular branch too, to which this little work is addreffed, has not been neglected; and it is an officer's own fault, if he is not sufficiently informed of his duty: books enough have been publifhed on the fubject, from thofe of Arrian, Onofander, and Vegetius, down to our modern fyftems of military difcipline, to fill a bookfeller's fhop; which any one may be convinced of, who will give himfelf the trouble of going to Charing-crofs. As the world in general does not feem to have become more wife or virtuous, in confequence of the numberlefs volumes that have been written for their inftruction and improvement; fo it does not appear that the different military publications within this laft century have added either to the knowledge or capacity of our generals, or to the good conduct or difcipline of our armies. Convinced as we are, then, of the
futility

futility of all former attempts, why enter on a freſh one? Does the author flatter himſelf, that he poſſeſſes more powers of perſuaſion than his brethren? No. But he has diſcovered the ſole reaſon why other adviſers have been ſo little attended to: namely, becauſe they have laid down a line of conduct in direct oppoſition to the inclination of their readers. Now, he has purſued a very different method; has endeavoured to ſeaſon his admonition to their appetites: and though he cannot expect to have ſo many readers, he doubts not but that his precepts and maxims will have more followers, than thoſe of Socrates or Epictetus, or any other moraliſt, who has undertaken the arduous taſk of reforming mankind.

Different maxims being adapted to the different ranks, he has addreſſed himſelf ſeparately to each, from the commander in chief of an army, down to the lowest order of non-commissioned officers. It may be judged a piece of presumption to offer instructions to commanders, who have grown grey in the service, and must be supposed to have already acquired sufficient experience and knowledge of their business. How far our generals may have had experience in their profession, or how far they may stand in need of advice, the author will not pretend to determine: he is, indeed, apt to imagine, that *some of them* are fully acquainted with his maxims, and have taken care, in the course of their command, to put them in practice. Such gentlemen may spare themselves the trouble of perusing them: he professes to write only for the instruction of the inexperienced and the uninformed.

ADVICE

A D V I C E

T O   T H E

O F F I C E R S

O F   T H E

B R I T I S H   A R M Y.

———◆———

C H A P T E R   I.

To General Officers, commanding in Chief.

A Commander in chief is to the army under his command, what the foul is to the body: it can neither think nor act without him; and, in short, is as perfect a non-entity without its commander, as a wife is without

her

her hufband. You muft, therefore, through pure good-will and affection for your troops, take care of your own facred perfon, and never expofe it to any dangers. You have not arrived at this rank without knowing the folly of knocking one's head againft a poft, when it can be avoided. When any fervice of danger is to be performed, you fhould fend your fecond in command, or fome inferior officer—but whomfoever you fend, if he fucceeds in the bufinefs, be fure to take all the merit of it to yourfelf.

You muft be as abfolute in your command, and as inacceffible to your troops, as the Eaftern fultans, who call themfelves the Lord's vicegerents upon earth. In fact, a commander in chief is greater than a fultan; for if he is not the Lord's vicegerent, he is the King's, which in the idea of a military man, is much better.

As

As no other perſon in your army is allowed to be poſſeſſed of a ſingle idea, it would be ridiculous, on any occaſion, to aſſemble a council of war, or, at leaſt, to be guided by their opinion : for, in oppoſition to yours, they muſt not truſt to the moſt evident perception of their ſenſes. It would be equally abſurd and unmilitary to conſult their convenience; even when it may be done without any detriment to the ſervice : that would be taking away the moſt effectual method of exerciſing their obedience, and of perfecting them in a very conſiderable branch of military diſcipline.

You have heard that ſecrecy is one of the firſt requiſites in a commander. In order, therefore, to get a name for this great military virtue, you muſt always be ſilent and ſullen, particularly at your own table; and I would adviſe you to ſecure your ſecrets the more effectually, by depoſiting

them

them in the safest place you can think
of; as, for instance, in the breast of
your wife or mistress.

Ignorance of your profession is like-
wise best concealed by solemnity and
silence, which pass for profound knowledge upon the generality of mankind.
A proper attention to these, together
with extreme severity, particularly in
trifles, will soon procure you the character of a good officer.

It is your duty to be attentive to
the public good, but not without some
regard to your own, in your dispen-
sation of favours. You must take
care never to advance an officer above
one step at a time, however brilliant
his merit, unless he be your relation:
for you must consider, that your ignorance in the higher branches of your
profession can only be covered by the
strictest attention to punctilio, and the
minutiæ of the service.

As

As you probably did not rife to your present diftinguifhed rank by your own merit, it cannot reafonably be expected that you fhould promote others on that fcore.

Above all, be careful never to promote an intelligent officer ; a brave, chuckle-headed fellow will do full as well to execute your orders. An officer, that has an iota of knowledge above the common run, you muft confider as your perfonal enemy ; for you may be fure he laughs at you and your manœuvres.

A principal part of your duty is to fee juftice diftributed among your troops. Military law being fo fummary and concife, you will not find this a difficult matter : but if, fimple as it is, you fhould be entirely unacquainted with it, you may fubftitute your own good will and pleafure—and that, in fact, muft be juftice ; for a

B   com-

commander in chief is as infallible as the Pope, and, being the King's reprefentative, he can do no wrong, any more than his royal mafter.

In diftributing juftice, you muft always incline a little to the ftrongeft fide. Thus, if a difpute happens between a field officer and a fubaltern, you muft, if poffible, give it in favour of the former.—Force is, indeed, the ruling principle in military affairs ; in conformity to which the French term their cannon, the *ratio ultima regum.*

Subordination being highly neceffary in an army, you muft take care to keep a proper diftance, firft between yourfelf and your fecretary, then between your fecretary and the general officers on the ftaff, and fo on to the laft link in the military chain.

Though you are not to allow fwearing in others, it being forbidden by
the

the articles of war, yet by introducing
a few oaths occafionally into your difcourfe, you will give your inferiors
fome idea of your courage ; efpecially
if you fhould be advanced in years :
for then they muft think you a dare-
devil indeed. I would recommend it
to you to make ufe of fome oath or
execration peculiar to yourfelf, in imitation of Queen Elizabeth and Captain
Bobadil ; as, "I hope to be damned,"
or any other equally expreffive of your
future wifhes or expectations.

Remember that eafe and convenience are apt to render foldiers effe-
minate ; witnefs Hannibal's army at
Capua. Never, therefore, let the troops
have comfortable quarters ; and as money, according to Horace, lowers a
man's courage, be fure to cut off every
emolument from your army, to prevent the impediment of a full purfe.
No perfons will behave fo defperately
in action as thofe who are tired of

their

their lives ; *Ibit eò quò vis qui zonam perdidit*—and the more you pinch the army under your command, the more you may appropriate to your own ufe : your country can afford to make you the handfomer allowance.

If you ferve under a miniftry, with whom œconomy is the word, make a great buftle and parade about retrenchment ; it will be prudent for you, likewife, to put it, in fome meafure, into practice ; but not fo as to extend to your own perquifites, or thofe of your dependents. Thefe favings are beft made out of the pay of the fubaltern officers and private foldiers ; who, being little able to bear it, will of courfe make much complaint of it, which will render your regard to œconomy the more confpicuous. And though your pay-mafter, or commiffary-general, may touch more than the amount of all that you retrench from the body of the army, no matter, if

you

you go fnacks with them: the public need know nothing about it, if they are but fnug, and learn how to keep their own fecrets.

Should the duties bear hard on any particular corps, never attend in the leaft to their reprefentations. Remonftrances are the forerunners of mutiny; and it is the higheft infult to your rank and command to infinuate that you are not infallible. This rule, however, may be difpenfed with, when the colonel or commanding-officer happens to be a peer or a man of great intereft.

Be fure to give out a number of orders. It will at leaft fhew the troops you do not forget them. The more trifling they are, the more it fhews your attention to the fervice; and fhould your orders contradict one another, it will give you an opportunity of altering them, and find subject for frefh regulations.

You

You will doubtlefs foon learn what to do with the fecret-fervice money. The gullibility of the minifters at home may perhaps induce them to believe, that this is all expended on fpies, on gaining intelligence, and other public interefts. So a part of it is, however fmall ; but there are other fervices equally fecret, and no lefs important—to the commander in chief, which muft be fupplied from this fund, efpecially if he has paffed his grand climacteric. In this you cannot be faid to cheat the public ; for you give them the real ftate of the ex-pence ; fo that there is no knavery or collufion in the matter.

You fhould have a clever fecretary to write your difpatches, in cafe you fhould not be fo well qualified your-felf. This gentleman may often ferve to get you out of a fcrape. You muft take pains fo to interlard your letters with technical terms, that neither the
public,

public, nor the minifter to whom they are addreffed, will underftand them; efpecially if the tranfactions you are defcribing be trivial: it will then give them an air of importance. This is conformable to the maxim in epic and dramatic poetry, of raifing the diction at times to cover the poverty of the fubject.

In your firft official letter you muft ingraft a tolerable number of French words, though there be English ones equally à propos, to give people an idea of your military talents: but then you fhould take care to keep up the fame fpirit of writing, otherwife they may imagine, that your abilities and your language are exhaufted together.

If upon fervice you have any ladies in your camp, be valiant in your converfation before them. There is nothing pleafes the ladies more than to hear

hear of ſtorming breaches, attacking the covert-way ſword in hand, and ſuch like martial exploits. This however I only recommend at night over the bottle : it cannot be expected that you ſhould be ſo valiant and blood-thirſty, upon mature deliberation, the next morning ; that, indeed, would be murder in cold blood.

Nothing is ſo commendable as gen-eroſity to an enemy. To follow up a victory, would be taking the advan-tage of his diſtreſs. It will be ſuffi-cient therefore for you to ſhew, that you can beat him when you think pro-per. Beſides, giving your enemy too ſevere a drubbing may put an end to the war, before you have feathered your neſt handſomely, and provided for your relations and dependents.

When you have occaſion to put into winter quarters or cantonments in an enemy's country, you ſhould place
your

your worſt troops, or thoſe you can leaſt depend upon, in the out-poſts: for if the enemy ſhould form the deſign of cutting them off, though he would be the more likely to ſucceed in it, yet the loſs, you know, is of the leſs conſequence to your army.

When an inferior general is to be detached upon an expedition, be ſure to ſend the moſt ignorant and inexperienced; for he ſtands the moſt in need of a leſſon.

You ſhould always act openly and fairly both with friends and foes. Never therefore ſteal a march, or lay in ambuſh; neither ſhould you fire upon or attack your enemy in the night. If you have read Pope's tranſlation of Homer, you may remember what Hector ſays, when about to fight with Ajax:

C   —*Open*

—Open be our fight, and bold each blow,
I steal no conquest from a noble foe.

If you are pursuing a retreating enemy, let him get a few days march a-head, to shew him that you have no doubt of being able to overtake him, when you set about it: and who knows but this proceeding may encourage him to stop? After he has retired to a place of security, you may then go in quest of him with your whole army.

It will be your own fault, if you do not make a fortune in the course of your command. When you come home, you have nothing to do but to enjoy *otium cum dignitate.* I would have you build a villa, and, in imitation of the great Duke of Marlborough, call it by the name of the most confiderable victory you have gained. If you have gained no victory, you may perhaps have taken some town

without

without ramparts or garrifon to defend it; which, if it has but a founding name, the public will give you as much credit for, as they would for Lifle, or Bergen-op-Zoom.

If you fhould ever be called into the fervice again, you will be too wife from your paft experience to go and expofe your old bones in Germany, America, or the Indies. So I would advife you to get the command of a camp or diftrict in old England; where you may enjoy all the pomp and parade of war, and, at the fame time, be tolerably fecure from thofe hard knocks, which your neceffities impelled you to rifk in your younger days.

CHAP.

CHAP. II.

To General Officers upon the Staff.

NOtwithſtanding your diſtinguiſhed rank in the army, whether you are a general, a lieutenant-general, a major-general, or a brigadier, you are no more to the commander in chief than a petty nabob is to the Great Mogul. If ever you wiſh to riſe a ſtep above your preſent degree, you muſt learn that maxim in the art of war, of currying favour with your ſuperiors; and you muſt not only cringe to the commander in chief himſelf, but you muſt take eſpecial care to keep in with his favourites, and dance attendance upon his ſecretary.

The more ſervility and fawning you practiſe towards thoſe above you, the more you have a right to exact from thoſe

thofe beneath you. You muſt therefore take care to let all the ſubalterns
know what reſpect is due to a general
officer.

If any appointments, ſuch as extra-
engineer, brigade-major, inſpector of
the works, or reſident-commiſſary,
happen to fall within your diſpoſal ; be
ſure to give them all in your own regiment, and to perſons who do not
want them, and are incapable of doing
the buſineſs. The leſs they are qualified to act, the greater the obliga-
tion to you, and the more evident the
demonſtration of your power. It will
ſhew that your favour is ſufficient to
enable a man to hold and to diſcharge
any office, however deficient his knowledge of the duties.

Nothing ſhews a general's attention
more than requiring a number of returns, particularly ſuch as it is difficult
to make with any degree of accuracy.
Let

Let your brigade-major, therefore, make out a variety of forms, the more red lines the better: as to the information they convey, that is immaterial; no one ever reads them, the chief ufe of them being to keep the adjutants and ferjeants in employment, and to make a perquifite to your valet-de chambre, who can fell them at the fnuff-fhop or to the grocer.

Whenever you are to review a regiment under your command, a fhort time before the review enquire the particular mode of exercife which the regiment has been accuftomed to, and oblige them to alter it for one quite different. This will fhew you are acquainted with the *minutiæ* or elements of the military fcience, as well as the *Grand Tactick*. Thus, if the regiment has been accuftomed to mark the cadence with the left foot, order them to do it with the right. Change the time of the manual; and make other
alte-

alterations of equal importance. It will occupy the attention of the foldier, and prevent him from falling into idlenefs, the fource of all evil.

If it fhould happen to rain when you are reviewing the troops, I would recommend it to you to provide yourfelf with a *parapluie,* and not imitate the conduct of an Irifh general, who, at a late review of the volunteers at Waterford, walked along the line with his hat off, during an inceffant fhower of rain. A general's perfon is to be fecured as well from the fury of the elements, as from that of the enemy's cannon. Befides, though we may admit the texture of your fkull to be equally fubftantial, yet as you have feen fome fervice, it may not require quite fo much cooling as that of the Hibernian general.

If you fhould command in a fortrefs that is laid fiege to, you muft referve
your

your fire to the laſt, that your ammunition may not be exhauſted : beſides
firing upon the enemy would ſo retard
their progreſs, that your garriſon might
be ſtarved into a capitulation, before
you could have a fair opportunity of
beating them.

But where an enemy thinks himſelf
able to beſiege you in a fortreſs, the
beſt and ſafeſt way to convince him of
his miſtake, is to march out and give
him battle.

You may ſometimes, however unfit
for it, be entruſted with the command
of an expedition. In this caſe, I dare
ſay you will take care to aſſume all
the privileges of a commander in chief :
I ſhall therefore refer you to ſome of
the hints addreſſed to that officer in the
laſt chapter.

CHAP.

CHAP. III.

To Aid-de-Camps of General Officers.

AN aid-de-camp is to his general what Mercury was to Jupiter, and what the jackal is to the lion. It is a poſt that very few can fill with credit, and requires parts and education to execute its duties with propriety. Miſtake me not; I do not mean that you are to puzzle your brain with Mathematicks, or ſpoil your eyes with poring over Greek and Latin. Nor is it neceſſary you ſhould underſtand military manœuvres, or even the manual exerciſe. It is the graces you muſt court, by means of their high prieſt, a dancing-maſter. Learn to make a good bow; that is the firſt grand eſſential; the next is to carve and hold the toaſt; and if you aſpire to great eminence, get a few French

D and

and German phrases by rote; these, besides giving you an air of learning, may induce people to suppose you have served abroad. Next to these accomplishments, the art of listening with a seeming attention to a long story, will be of great use to you; particularly if your general is old and has served in former wars, or has accidentally been present at any remarkable siege or battle. On all occasions take an opportunity of asking him some question, that may lead him to describe the particulars of those transactions.

You are not only the Sir Clement Cottrell at the general's levee, but you must also act as his *Nomenclator* abroad. Whenever you whisper in his ear the name of any officer, you should at the same time contrive, if possible, to drop some little hint of his character, or some anecdote, though it should be in the officer's favour. This will give
the

the general an idea of your extenſive knowledge.

If your general keeps a girl, it is your duty to ſquire her to all public places, and to make an humble third of a party at whiſt or quadrille; but be ſure never to win: if you ſhould be ſo unlucky as to have a good hand, when againſt your general, renounce, or by ſome other means contrive to make as little of it as you can.

When your general invites any ſub-alterns to his table, it will be unbe-coming your dignity to take any no-tice of them. If there are any field-officers or captains invited, you may condeſcend to chatter and hob-nob with *them*. You may, indeed, be under the neceſſity of carving for the ſub-alterns, that being your immediate of-fice; in which caſe, help them to the coarſeſt bits, and take care that they

are

are vifited by the bottle as feldom as poffible.

Whenever the general fends you with a meffage in the field, though ever fo trifling, gallop as faft as you can up to and againft the perfon, to whom it is addreffed. Should you ride over him, it will fhew your alertnefs in the performance of your duty.

In delivering the meffage be as concife as poffible, no matter whether you are underftood or not, and gallop back again as faft as you came. To appear the more warlike, you fhould ride with your fword drawn ; but take care you do not cut your horfe's ear off.

When the general reviews a regiment, it is your bufinefs to receive the returns. Juft as the officer paffes by, contrive to run againft him, fo as to make him lofe the ftep, and put him out

out at leaſt, if you cannot throw the whole diviſion into diſorder.

In coming with orders to a camp, gallop through every ſtreet of the different regiments, particularly if the ground be ſoft and boggy. A great man ſhould always leave ſome tracks behind him.

Make it your buſineſs, in common, with the chaplain and adjutant, to collect all the news and ſcandal of the camp or garriſon, and report it to your general. But be careful not to loſe any particulars, eſpecially if any officers of the general's regiment are concerned : this will prevent your being rivalled in his confidence.

You ſhould always aſſume a myſterious air; and if any one aſks you the moſt trifling queſtion, ſuch as, whether the line will be out at exerciſe tomorrow? or any other matter of equal im-

importance, never give a direct anfwer; but look grave, and affectedly
turn the difcourfe to fome other fubject. If a fubaltern fhould only venture to afk you, what it is o'clock?
you muft not inform him, in order to
fhew that you are fit to be entrufted
with fecrets.

In a word, let your deportment be
haughty and infolent to your inferiors,
humble and fawning to your fuperiors,
folemn and diftant to your equals.

CHAP.

C H A P. IV.

*To   Colonels   and   Lieutenant-Colonels
commanding corps.*

AS foon as you have arrived at the command of a regiment, you will form your conduct upon the model of your fuperiors, and be as defpotic in your little department as the great Cham of Tartary. When giving orders to your regiment on the parade, or marching at the head of it, you will doubtlefs, feel as bold as a cock, and look as fierce as a lion ; yet, when the commander in chief, or any other general officer approaches, it muft all fubfide into the meeknefs of the lamb and the obfequioufnefs of the fpaniel.

You are to confider yourfelf as the father of your corps, and muft take care to exercife a paternal authority
over

over it: as a good father does not
fpare the rod, fo fhould not a commanding officer fpare the cat-of-nine-
tails.

It is your duty alfo to be very attentive to the good of your regiment, and
to keep a watchful eye to its advantage,
except when it clafhes with your own.
If you have intereft with the commander in chief, always be careful to
fecure yourfelf good winter quarters;
and if you have an inclination to any
particular town, either from having a
miftrefs there, or any other good caufe,
you need not mind marching your
regiment two or three hundred miles
to it. Though it will fatigue the foldiers and drain the officers' purfes, they
will not dare to grumble at it, but will
be happy, I am fure, to oblige their
commander. Soldiers, you know, are
merely intended for your ufe and convenience, juft as the people are created
for

for the pleasure of the kings who go-
vern them.

But if there are any of your field-officers, or others, who have more interest
at Court than yourself, you must direct
your march where they think proper.
I know an instance of a major, who,
being fond of the sports of the field,
got his regiment ordered from their
encampment in Kent into winter quarters in Cornwall. Hearing, however,
when the regiment had got to Exeter
in its way, that there was better shoot-
ing, as well as hunting, in Hampshire,
he immediately posts to the War-office,
and gets the order countermanded.
They are accordingly faced to the right-
about, and marched back again to the
New Forest ; where they arrive, the
soldiers without shoes, and the officers
without any inclination for hunting.
Thus had they the pleasure of seeing
the world, and of marching two hundred miles and back again, to the

great

great advantage of the publicans, and
the farmers' pigs and fowls on the
road—becauſe their major was a
ſportſman.

When promoted to the command of
a regiment from ſome other corps,
ſhew them that they were all in the
dark before, and, overturning their
whole routine of diſcipline, introduce
another as different as poſſible; I will
not ſuppoſe of your own—you may not
have genius enough for that : but if
you can only contrive to vamp up ſome
old exploded ſyſtem, it will have all
the appearance of novelty to thoſe,
who have never practiſed it before :
the few who have, will give you credit for having ſeen a great deal of
ſervice.

If your regiment ſhould not be provided with a band of muſic, you ſhould
immediately perſuade the captains to
raiſe one. This, you know, is kept
at

at their expence, whilſt you reap the principal benefit; for beſides keeping them always with your own company, and treating them as your own private band, they will, if properly managed, as by lending them to private parties, aſſemblies, &c. ſerve to raiſe you a conſiderable intereſt among the gentlemen of the country, and, what is of more conſequence, among the ladies.

You cannot take too much pains to maintain ſubordination in your corps. The ſubalterns of the Britiſh army are but too apt to think themſelves gentlemen; a miſtake which it is your buſineſs to rectify. Put them, as often as you can, upon the moſt diſagreeable and ungentlemanly duties; and endeavour by every means to bring them upon a level with the ſubaltern officers of the German armies.

Never ſpeak kindly to a non-commiſſion officer. An auſtere and diſtant

beha-

behaviour gives them an elevated idea of your dignity ; and if it does not tend to make them love you, it will at leaſt cauſe them to fear you, which is better.

Whenever any overſight or miſdemeanour, however trivial, is reported to have been committed by an officer, order him under an immediate arreſt, without giving yourſelf the trouble of an enquiry. If he is an old offender, you ſhould conſider him as irreclaimable, and releaſe him ſoon after. But if he has in general conducted himſelf with propriety, be ſure to bring him to a court-martial. This will eſtabliſh your character with the commander in chief, by ſhewing that you are determined to ſupport diſcipline, and that the ſmalleſt offence will not eſcape your notice. Beſides, it is more inexcuſable in a good officer ; for he has not the power of habit to plead as an alleviation : and you know

know it will be beſt to nip his vices in
the bud.

Never ſtir without an orderly ſer-
jeant, particularly when you ride
through a town, or from one regiment
to another. If you have no other uſe
for him, he will ſerve to hold your
horſe when you diſmount.

When the regiment is on the march,
gallop from front to rear as often as
poſſible, eſpecially if the road is duſty.
Never paſs through the intervals, but
charge through the centre of each platoon or diviſion. The cry of—*open to
the right and left—incline to the right*
—marks your importance: and it is
diverting enough to duſt a parcel of
fellows, already half choaked, and to
ſee a poor devil of a ſoldier, loaded
like a jack-aſs, endeavouring to get
out of the way. In your abſence, the
ſame liberty may be taken by the adjutant.

If

If on fervice you are appointed to
the command of any garrifon or poft,
guard every part except that by which
the enemy is moft likely to approach :
for if you prevent his coming, you can
have no opportunity of fhewing your
valour. Thefe parts you may recon-
noitre yourfelf ; and if you fhould be
taken, you will at any rate get the
character of an alert officer, having
been the firft to difcover the enemy.

The command of five or fix hundred men will give you fome idea of
your own confequence ; and you will
of courfe look down upon all but your
fuperiors in the army, and gentlemen
of high rank and fortune. Though
your father may have been a pedlar
or an excifeman, you will entertain a
hearty contempt for all *bourgeois* ; and
though your education may have been
confined to reading, writing, and the
four firft rules in Arithmetick, yet you
are

are to confider every man as an ignorant and illiterate fellow, who knows
not how to manœuvre a battalion.

CHAP.

CHAP. V.

To Majors.

EVERY one knows it is the major's bufinefs to exercife the regiment on horfeback. It appears, therefore, that the principal, and indeed the only, requifites for this office, are, the lungs of a *Stentor*, and a good feat in the faddle.

If you were ignorant of your bufinefs when promoted to this poft, you need not give yourfelf much trouble to acquire a knowledge of it. The ftudy of the manœuvres you may leave to the ferjeant-major, and that of the exercife to the drill-ferjeants : all that it is neceffary for you to learn, is how to drop the point of your fword.

When-

Whenever you are to exercife the regiment, get the adjutant or ferjeant-major to write out on a fmall card the words of command in the proper order : and if you cannot retain the manœuvres in your head, you may at leaft keep them in your hat ; which will anfwer the fame purpofe.

But however convenient it may be to keep your card in the crown of your hat, when you exercife the regiment on foot, it will not do quite fo well on horfeback. In this cafe you may fix it on the faddle or holfter-pipe, or, which I would rather recommend, on the cap of the orderly drummer : but then you muft take care that he fticks as clofe to you as *Eo*, *Meo*, and *Areo*.

In exercifing the regiment, call out frequently to fome of the moft attentive men and officers to drefs, cover, or fomething of that nature : the lefs they are reprehenfible, the greater will

F   your

your difcernment appear to the by-
ftanders, in finding out a fault invifible
to them.

When it is your turn to be field-
officer of the day in camp, be fure to
keep the picquets waiting as long as
you can, particularly if it fhould rain:
this will accuftom the foldiers to ftand
the weather, and will make them glad
to fee you. When you come, contrive by fpurring your horfe to make
him prance, fo that he may be near
overturning the captain of the picquet;
by which means you will get the credit
of riding a fpirited charger. But this
muft be done with caution; I knew a
major, who, by an attempt of this
kind, wound up a fpirit in his horfe
that he could not lay, but was himfelf
depofited in the dirt.

In going the rounds in the night,
do not fail to keep the ferjeant and efcort in a good round trot. This will
pre-

prevent their catching cold, and may be done without the leaſt inconvenience, if you are on horſeback.

Be ſure to report any non-commiſſion officer's guard, where the counterſign is pronounced wrong; eſpecially, if it be a foreign word; that will demonſtrate your knowledge of the language. That you may have ſome one to find fault with, hide your lanthorn, and ſteal upon them as privately as poſſible: but in viſiting a quarter-guard, take care to give ſufficient notice of your approach; and, ſhould the officer be aſleep, abſent, or drunk, it would be ill-natured to mention it, and would beſides injure the ſervice, by making the corps of officers leſs reſpectable.

You muſt leave all the troubleſome parts of your buſineſs to your deputy, the adjutant—for you have a property in him, as well as the commanding of-

ficer.

ficer. Your authority, however, extends only to the field; the other can command his services also in the closet. I take it for granted, then, that you will contrive to throw all the detail upon his shoulders; and shall therefore proceed to give him a few directions for his conduct.

C H A P.

CHAP. VI.

To the Adjutant.

AN adjutant is a wit *ex officio*, and finds many ſtanding jokes annexed to his appointment. It is on the happy application of theſe that his character depends. Thus, for example, when the men loſe the ſtep, you may obſerve, that their legs move like thoſe before a hoſier's ſhop in windy weather; if, in the platoon exerciſe, they do not come down to the *preſent* together, that they perform the motions juſt as they were born, one after the other. In ſhort, by attending a little to the converſation of the wags among the non-commiſſion officers and ſoldiers, you may ſoon form a very pretty collection; which certainly muſt be ſterling, as they have ſtood the teſt of perhaps a century.

Read-

Reading and writing are very neceffary accomplifhments for an adjutant.
If you cannot fpell, you fhould keep
Entick's dictionary in your pocket;
but it will be of little ufe, if you know
not the meaning of the words : fo it
will be beft for you to get the ferjeant-
major, or fome other intelligent non-
commiffion officer, if there be fuch in
the corps, to write your orders, letters, &c.

If you are deficient in knowledge of
your duty, the word of command given
in a boatfwain's tone of voice, with a
tolerable affurance, and the dextrous
ufe of your oaken fapling, will carry
you through till you get a fmattering
of your bufinefs.

The manœuvres performed by a regiment are merely intended to fhew
the fkill of the adjutant ; for, I apprehend, no other manœuvres are ufed
upon fervice, but to march up to the
                                    enemy,

enemy, when the battalion feels bold,
and to run away, when it is not
in a fighting humour. All manœuvres ſhould therefore be calculated
to aſtoniſh the ſpectators, and the
more confuſed and intricate they
are, the better. A good adjutant
ſhould be able to play as many tricks
with a regiment, as Breſlaw can with
a pack of cards. There is one in particular that I would recommend, namely, that of diſperſing and falling in
again by the colours ; which you will
find extremely uſeful, whenever you
contrive to club, or otherwiſe to con-
fuſe, the battalion.

Whenever the colonel or commanding officer is on the parade, you ſhould
always ſeem in a hurry, and the oftener
you run or gallop from right to left,
the more aſſiduous will you appear :
laying your rattan now and then over
the head, or acroſs the face, of ſome
old ſoldier, for being ſtiff through in-
firmity,

firmity, will get you the character of a fmart adjutant.

Should you make a miftake in telling off a divifion, fhift the blame from your own fhoulders, by abufing the ferjeant or corporal of the divifion; and when, at any time, there is a blundering or confufion in a manœuvre, ride in amongft the foldiers, and lay about you from right to left. This will convince people that it was not your fault.

Be fure to liften to every piece of fcandal refpecting the commanding officer, and tell him of it the firft opportunity. Should none be thrown out, it might not be amifs to invent fome. If he keeps a lady, wait upon her with the utmoft refpect, be her *chaperon* to all public places, feed her dog, and. fcratch the poll of her parrot—but take care that your attention to the lady does not make her keeper jealous.

This

This might be of bad confequence to you.

Never fuffer your rofter to be queftioned, and though it fhould be wrong, never condefcend to alter it. The rofter is the adjutant's log-book, which he is to manage as will be moft conducive to his own private views. If you fhould therefore have a pique againft any officer, you fhould contrive to fend him upon the moft dangerous and difagreeable duties; and thefe he cannot in honour decline: for you know, according to military rules, an officer muft do the duty the adjutant orders him on firft, and remonftrate afterwards. Probably he will never return —but if he fhould, it will not require much dexterity to acquit yourfelf, if you are upon a proper footing with the commanding officer. His friends themfelves cannot fay that you do him a real injury: for you put him in a way of being handfomely provided for, and

G   of

of paying his debts in a foldierlike manner.

If you fhould be appointed adjutant to a regiment of militia, endeavour, as foon as you join the corps, to give the officers an idea of your military talents, by making it appear that you have feen a vaft deal of fervice. Talk of your campaigns in Germany, and America, of the roafting you have experienced in the Eaft and Weft Indies, and the cold of Newfoundland and Canada. If you have been in none of thofe places, no matter; they cannot difpute it, for you may fwear none of them have been there.

CHAP.

CHAP. VII.

To the Quarter-Master.

THE ſtanding maxim of your office is to receive whatever is offered you, or you can get hold of, but not to part with any thing you can keep. Your ſtore-room muſt reſemble the lion's den;

Multa te advorſum ſpectantia, pauca re-*trorſum*.

Live and let live, is alſo another golden rule, which you muſt remember and practiſe, particularly reſpecting the contractor for bread and forage; who, if he is grateful, will not forget your kindneſs : whence you may find it in reality a *golden* rule.

Obſerve

Obferve the fame with refpect to ftraw and wood. It is mechanical, and unbecoming a gentleman, to be weighing them like a cheefemonger. When the foldiers are receiving ftraw for the hofpital, order them to drop a trufs or two at your hut in the rear. This will lighten their burthen, and make the tafk lefs toilfome. The fame may be done with the wood for the hofpital; and the fick, efpecially the feverifh, have little need of fire in fummer.

Whenever any regimental ftores are fent to the regiment, be fure to unpack them immediately, and feize upon the packages as your own perquifite. At the conclufion of a campaign take care alfo to fecure the tents of the rear and quarter-guards.

When your regiment is ordered out of barracks, as you are the principal depredator, it will be neceffary for you

to

to get out of the way firſt. Go off
therefore the day before, under the
pretence of providing quarters for the
regiment; by which means you will get
out of the barrack-maſter's clutches;
whom you need not previouſly be at
the trouble of ſettling with; but leave
him to do it, as well as he can, with the
quarter-maſter of the corps that is to
march into the barracks.

You need not mind, whether the
proviſion iſſued to the ſoldiers be
good or bad. If it were always good,
they would get too much attached to
eating to be good ſoldiers,—and as a
proof that this gormandiſing is not military, you will not find in a gallant
army of 50,000 men a ſingle fat man,
unleſs it be a quarter-maſter, or a
quarter-maſter-ſerjeant.

If the ſoldiers complain of the bread,
taſte it, and ſay, better men have eat
much worſe. Talk of the *bompernicle*,
or

or black rye bread of the Germans, and
fwear you have feen the time when you
would have jumped at it.   Call them a
fet of grumbling rafcals, and threaten
to confine them for mutiny.   This,
if it does not convince them of the
goodnefs of the bread, will at leaft
frighten them, and make them take it
quietly.

If any good rum or brandy fhould be
delivered to you from the commiffary's
ftores for the foldiers, or wine (which
might poffibly happen) for the hofpital, you fhould rectify what was certainly a miftake in the contractors, by
appropriating it to your own ufe, and
fubftituting fome of an inferior qua-
lity,—unlefs the commanding officer
fhould infift upon this as his perquifite.
By fo doing you will prevent them
from becoming dainty: for fhould
they once tafte fuch choice liquor, it
might tend to make them difcontented
with their common allowance.

Always

Always keep a horſe or two. It would be hard, if you could not have hay and corn enough to maintain them, conſidering how much paſſes through your hands.

When you go before the regiment to take quarters, be ſure to get drunk with the quarter-maſter of the regiment that you are to relieve. Your quarter-maſter-ſerjeant may draw the billets, receive the ſtore-rooms, &c.; and if he alſo ſhould get drunk with his bro-ther quarter-maſter-ſerjeant, it is no great matter:—let the ſoldiers wait; it will prevent their going into their quarters in a heat.

The quarter-maſter is conſidered as the ſteward of the colonel—You muſt therefore be careful to diſcharge your duty like a good ſteward, who has ſuch a regard for his maſter, as to extend it even to his ſervants; amongſt whom, he does not forget himſelf; but, knowing

ing the value of his own services, takes
care to secure to himself a due propor-
tion ; merely that his master may not
be charged with ingratitude. You
must on all occasions endeavour to in-
culcate the doctrines of witchcraft and
inchantment : it will be difficult to account on other principles for the sud-
den and frequent disappearance of various articles out of your magazine.

CHAP.

CHAP. VIII.

To the Surgeon.

A Regimental furgeon muſt invert the apothecaries' maxim, of drenching the patient with medicines; and muſt be a great advocate for leaveing nature to her own operations; unleſs he has diſcovered ſome ſuch uſeful and unchargeable *panacæa* as Doctor Sangrado's.

The great ſecret of your profeſſion is the art of ſubſtitution. By this you may provide yourſelf with medicines, the produce of your own native ſoil, which will rival in excellence the moſt expenſive articles from the Levant or the Indies. Thus chalk will do for crab's eyes, or any teſtaceous powder, oil of turpentine, for balſam of capivi, and oak bark, for Peruvian.—By the way, it would be inconſiſtent with your

H   cha-

character, as a good proteſtant, to encourage thoſe thieves the Jeſuits, by
uſing any of their medicines ; and you
have a further inducement, as a patriot,
to promote the conſumption of Britiſh
commodities, in preference to thoſe of
ſtrangers.

By this art of ſubſtitution, a comfortable bowl of punch may, on an
emergency, be compounded out of the
medicine cheſt. Honey will ſerve for
ſugar, vitriol affords a good acid, and
ſpirits of wine will do for rum or brandy.

As the ſoldiers are apt to be extremely troubleſome to the ſurgeon of
a regiment, and your mate may be ignorant, or too much of a gentleman,
take a private man out of the ranks,
and inſtruct him to act as your deputy.
The principal part of his buſineſs will
be to bleed, and dreſs ſore backs ;——
as ſoon as he is expert in theſe, you
may teach him to draw teeth ; which
is

is foon acquired—but then he muſt take care, in performing this operation, to give the men a confounded pull;—in order to ſhew them, that he is not a common tooth-drawer.

You may afterwards teach him the method of making up your preſcriptions. If he ſhould miſtake arſenic for cream of tartar, it is not your fault, and it is a hundred to one it will never be found out; and ſhould he in bleeding divide an artery, or lame a ſoldier, it is an accident, you know, that might have happened to the firſt ſurgeon in England.

If a patient ſeems likely to coſt you ſome trouble or medicine, report him incurable, and perſuade the colonel or commanding officer to diſcharge him.

Whenever you are ignorant of a ſoldier's complaint, you ſhould firſt take a little blood from him, and then give

him

him an emetic and a cathartic—to
which you may add a blister. This will
serve, at least, to diminish the number
of your patients.

Keep two lancets; a blunt one for
the soldiers, and a sharp one for the
officers : this will be making a proper
distinction between them.

If it is the custom of your regiment
for the soldiers to be cured of the vene-
real disease *gratis*, give yourself but
little concern about them, and be sure
to treat them as roughly as possible.
Tenderness towards patients of that
kind, is only an encouragement of
vice; and if you make a perfect and
speedy cure, they will soon forget the
inconveniences of the disorder: where-
as if they carry some *mementos* about
them, it will make them thenceforward
the more cautious. If you are paid for
it, you may observe nearly the same
conduct towards them ; for experience
shews,

ſhews, that cure them as often as you will, they ſoon contract it again ; ſo it is only ſo much labour and medicine thrown away. Beſides, as the ladies of the camp or garriſon are pretty much in common, theſe men may, by circulating the diſorder, procure you ſome practice among the officers.

Order your deputy carefully to pre- ſerve all the poultices uſed in the hoſ- pital.   They may go in part of his wages ; and he will be ſure to find a purchaſer among the ſutlers in camp, or the poulterers in town.   In this, however, you may meet with ſome op- poſition ; for it may be conſidered by the nurſe as a part of her perquiſites.

If any of the ſoldiers' wives or chil- dren happen to be taken ill, never give them any aſſiſtance.   You receive no pence from them, and you know *ex ni- hilo nihil fit*.   Excuſe yourſelf by ſay- ing, which you probably may with
much

much truth, that you have not medicines enough for the foldiers.

When the flux or any putrid diforder reigns in the camp or garrifon, be fure to procure wine for the ufe of your hofpital. But confider, altho' it is a great anti-feptic, it is alfo inflammatory; and therefore to be given fparingly to your patients. The remainder may ferve to treat your brother furgeons and mates with; and indeed will be neceffary to prevent your taking any infectious diforder.

Inoculation affords a pretty comfortable *douceur* to gentlemen of your profeffion, a guinea per head being allowed by Government for that operation. But as it is only to be performed with the foldier's confent, you fhould recollect, that the common people are commonly blind to their own intereft, and therefore perfuade as many as you can to agree to what is fo much for
their

their advantage. If you fhould by miftake inoculate a foldier that has already had the infection, it will not be attended with any ill confequences; and if you fhould perform the operation on one who is fickening with the diftemper, it will not in the leaft add to its malignity.

When a foldier receives a wound in a leg or an arm, immediately fix the tourniquet, though there may be the faireft profpect of preferving the limb. This will fave you a world of trouble, and your patient a vaft deal of pain. You will befides do him a moft effential benefit, in fending him to enjoy the repofe of Chelfea hofpital, inftead of being dragged from one place to another, at the perpetual rifk of having his brains knocked out : partial evil is univerfal good ; and the facrifice of a limb may eventually be the prefervation of all the reft of his carcafe.

C H A P.

C H A P. IX.

To the Chaplain.

THE chaplain is a character of
no fmall importance in a regiment, though many gentlemen of the
army think otherwife. Yet if you are
not more fuccefsful in the cure of the
foul, than the furgeon is in that of the
body, I muft confefs your 6s. 8d. a
day would be a judicious faving. You
have fuch hardened finners to deal
with, that your office is rather an un-
gracious one ; but though the officers
and foldiers are in general irreclaimable, the women of the regiment may
perhaps be worked on with better
effect.

If you are ambitious of being
thought a good preacher by your fcar-
let flock, you muft take care that your
fer-

fermons be very fhort. That is the
firft excellence in the idea of a foldier.

Never preach any practical morality
to the regiment. That would be only
throwing away your time. To a man
they all know, as well as you do, that
they ought not to get drunk or com-
mit adultery: but preach to them on
the Trinity, the attributes of the
Deity, and other myftical and ab-
ftrufe fubjects, which they may never
before have thought or heard of. This
will give them a high idea of your
learning: befides, your life might otherwife give the lie to your preaching.

You may indulge yourfelf in fwearing, and talking bawdy as much as
you pleafe; this will fhew you are not
a ftiff high prieft. Moreover, example being more effectual than precept,
it will point out to the young officers
the ugly and ungentlemanly appearance of the practice, and thereby de-

I   ter

ter them; just as the antients used to make their slaves get drunk, in order to render that vice odious to their children.

Remember that it is your duty, in common with the adjutant, to report all the little scandal of the regiment to the commanding officer; whose favour you should omit no means to court and procure. This will set you above the malicious jokes of the young subalterns.

If any one offends you by rivalling you in your amours, or debauching your girl, call him out to give you the satisfaction of a gentleman: for though the christian religion and the articles of war both forbid duelling; yet these restraints are not regarded by men of spirit.

If you understand any Greek or Latin, take every occasion of introducing

ducing fentences of them, tho' they
be as little to the purpofe and as unintelligible as thofe of Partridge or
Lingo: and if you fhould confound
the lines of the Æneid with thofe of
Propria quæ maribus, it will not hurt
your charaćter for learning in the eyes
of the officers: for it is ten to one
that none of them underftand a word
about the matter.

As the articles of war are fo very
careful in protećting you from injury,
you may prefume a little upon it, in
order to fupport the dignity of the
clerical charaćter: and if any of the
officers fhould give you juft caufe of
offence, as by laughing at you in your
cups, or beating your dog, complain
of the giddinefs of youth, and of the
little refpećt fhewn to religion in thefe
licentious times.

If you are not already expert at it,
it will be highly proper for you to

learn

learn to carve. This accomplifhment
has been from time immemorial a neceffary appendage to the priefthood.
Thus in former ages the priefts ufed to
cut up the lambs, goats, and other
animals, that were facrificed to the
Deity upon the altar : but modern re-
finement has improved upon the practice, and now the churchmen are
unanimoufly of opinion, that the Deity
is equally gratified with the favoury
fumes of good roaft and boiled.

At the mefs always keep two plates ;
one for immediate ufe, and the other
to fecure a flice of pye, pudding, or
other choice bit, that might vanifh
whilft you were eating what you had
before you. This will be a very neceffary precaution, if you have many
young fubalterns in the mefs ; among
whom thofe articles, like many other
good things of this world, are extremely tranfitory.

Should

Should you want to provide yourfelf with a deputy, be not over fcru-
pulous refpecting his character or
morals. It would be a pity that he
fhould be well difpofed ; for he would
be fure foon to get fpoiled among the
officers. It is not neceffary even that
he fhould underftand Englifh : for, as
they never liften to his harangues,
any other language, or compound of
languages, whether Cambrian, Erfe,
French, or Irifh, will juft anfwer the
fame purpofe.

When any old campaigners bore the
mefs with their long ftories of marches
or battles, be fure to retort upon them
with a hiftory of your exploits at college,—of the defperate combats you
have had with the *raffs*, the fweating
you were obliged to go through in
the pig-market, and your hair-breadth
efcapes from the proctor's clutches—
and though you may never have been
at college at all, yet you muft not fail
to

to make people believe, that you have
taken a mafter's degree at leaft, in
one of the univerfities.

CHAP.

CHAP. X.

To the Paymaſter.

YOUR's is as ſnug an office as any; particularly when the regiment is upon foreign ſervice; but if you have give ſecurity, or have a commiſſion to anſwer for your miſcarriages, you muſt take care to go on fair and ſoftly.

Make your accounts as intricate as you can, and, if poſſible, unintelligible to every one but yourſelf; leſt, in caſe you ſhould be taken priſoner, your papers might give information to the enemy.

Always grumble and make difficulties, when officers go to you for money that is due to them; when you are obliged to pay them, endeavour to

make

make it appear granting them a favour, and tell them they are lucky dogs to get it. I dare ſay, they would be of the ſame way of thinking, if you had it in your power to withhold it.

Be careful to keep up a right un-derſtanding with the agent ; and be mindful of the old ſaying, When * * * fall out ———— &c.

You muſt alſo keep upon good terms with the commanding officer ; which will be no difficult matter, if he is extravagant and needy. Juſt before muſter-day get leave, or take it, to be abſent from the regiment, and pretend that it is upon the buſi-neſs of your office, as to receive mo-ney, get caſh for bills, ſettle with the agent, &c. The longer you ſtay away the better, and the more to your credit : for ſhewing people that they cannot do without you, will give them a high idea of your importance ;

and

you will be fure of a hearty welcome on your return.

Always clofe your accounts with *errors excepted;* and, as you give people this caution, it is but fair that the miftakes fhould be all in your own favour.

I know not whence they call your monthly pay-rolls *abſtracts;* unleſs it be confidering them as abftracted from all found arithmetick, and juft calculation.

When you pay any allowance to the officers and foldiers beyond the ufual fubfiftence, be fure to deduct fix-pence in the pound for your friend the agent; who certainly deferves that perquifite, for his great trouble and rifk in taking care of the money for you fo long: efpecially, as you may fwear he has not put it out to intereft.

K   C H A P.

CHAP. XI.

To Young Officers.

THOSE who are unacquainted with the fervice may perhaps imagine, that this chapter is addreſſed to the ſubalterns only—but a little knowledge of the preſent ſtate of the Britiſh forces will ſoon convince them, that it comprehends not only the greateſt part of the captains, but alſo many of the field officers, of the army.

The firſt article we ſhall conſider is your dreſs ; a taſte in which is the moſt diſtinguiſhing mark of a military genius, and the principal characteriſtic of a good officer.

Ever ſince the days of Antient Piſtol, we find, that a large and broad-rimmed beaver has been peculiar to heroes.

heroes. A hat of this kind worn over your right eye, with two large dangling taſſels, and a proportionate cockade and feather, will give you an air of courage and martial gallantry.

The faſhion of your clothes muſt depend on that ordered in the corps ; that is to ſay, muſt be in direct oppoſition to it : for it would ſhew a deplorable poverty of genius, if you had not ſome ideas of your own in dreſs.

Your croſs belt ſhould be broad, with a huge blade pendent to it—to which you may add a dirk and a bayonet, in order to give you the more tremendous appearance.

Thus equipped you ſally forth, with your colours, or chitterlin, advanced and flying ; and I think it will be beſt in walking through the ſtreets, particularly if they are narrow, to carry your ſword in your right hand. For

K 2   beſides

befides its having a handfome and military appearance, the pommel of the fword will ferve to open you a free paffage, by fhoving it in the guts of every one who does not give way. He muft be a bold man who will venture to oppofe you; as by your drefs he cannot in reafon expect the leaft quarter. We are told that the Janiffaries never wear their fwords but upon duty; a practice more becoming Turks than Chriftians.

When you vifit your friends either in town or country, or make an excurfion to any other place where your regiment is not known, immediately mount two epaulettes, and pafs yourfelf for a grenadier officer.

Never wear your uniform in quarters, when you can avoid it. A green or a brown coat fhews you have other clothes befide your regimentals, and likewife that you have courage to dif-
obey

obey a ſtanding order. If you have not an entire ſuit, at leaſt mount a pair of black breeches, a round hat, or ſomething unregimental and unmilitary.

If you belong to a meſs, eat with it as ſeldom as poſſible, to let folks ſee you want neither money nor credit. And when you do, in order to ſhew that you are uſed to good living, find fault with every diſh that is ſet on the table, damn the wine, and throw the plates at the meſs-man's head.

If the dinner is not ſerved up immediately on your ſitting down, draw circles with your fork on the table ; cut the table-cloth ; and, if you have pewter plates, ſpin them on the point of your fork, or do ſome other miſchief, to puniſh the fellow for making you wait.

On coming into the regiment, perhaps the major or adjutant will adviſe you to learn the manual, the ſalute, or other

other parts of the exercife; to which
you may anfwer, that you do not want
to be drill-ferjeant or corporal—or that
you purchafed your commiffion, and
did not come into the army to be made
a machine of.

It will alfo be perfectly needlefs for
you to confult any treatife of military
difcipline, or the regulations for the
army. Dry books of tactics are beneath the notice of a man of genius,
and it is a known fact, that every Bri-
tifh officer is infpired with a perfect
knowledge of his duty, the moment he
gets his commiffion; and if he were
not, it would be fufficiently acquired
in *converfaziones* at the main-guard or
the grand futler's. Thus a general officer, who had never before feen a
day's fervice beyond the limits of Black-
heath or Wimbledon-common, being
ordered abroad, lands in America or
Germany a *factus imperator*, though
by very different means from thofe of
Lucul-

Lucullus. If you have a turn for reading, or find it neceſſary to kill in that manner the tedious hours in camp or garriſon, let it be ſuch books as warm the imagination and inſpire to military atchievements, as, *The Woman of Pleaſure*, *Crazy Tales*, *Rocheſter's Poems*; if you aim at ſolid inſtruction and uſeful knowledge, you muſt ſtudy *Lord Cheſterfield's Letters*, or *Truſler's Politeneſs*; if you have a turn for natural philoſophy, you may peruſe *Ariſtotle's Maſter-piece*; and the *Trials for Adultery* will afford you a fund of hiſtorical and legal information.

If there ſhould be a ſoberly diſpoſed perſon, or, in other words, a fellow of no ſpirit, in the corps, you muſt not only *bore* him conſtantly at the meſs, but ſhould make uſe of a kind of practical wit to torment him. Thus you may force open his doors, break his windows, damage his furniture, and put wh——s in his bed; or in camp

throw

throw squibs and crackers into his tent at night, or loosen his tent-cords in windy weather. Young gentlemen will never be at a loss for contrivances of this nature.

Be sure also to stigmatize every officer, who is attentive to his duty, with the appellation of *Martinet;* and say he has been bitten by a mad adjutant. This will discourage others from knowing more than yourself, and thereby keep you upon an equality with them.

When ordered for duty, always grumble and question the roster. This will procure you the character of one that will not be imposed on. At a field day, be sure not to fall in before the regiment is told off and proved; and then come upon the parade, buttoning your gaiters, or putting on some part of your dress. Observe the same when for guard:—making 20 or 30 men wait, shews you are somebody.

When-

Whenever you mount guard, invite all your friends to the guard-room; and not only get drunk yourself, but make your company drunk alfo; and then fing, and make as much noife as poffible. This will fhew the world the difference between an officer and a private man; fince the latter would be flayed alive for the leaft irregularity upon duty.

Though it may, on fome occafions, be proper and becoming a military man, to be watchful and fit up all night, as in drinking, gaming, at a mafquerade, &c. yet it would be an intolerable bore on guard; and, if near an enemy, and liable to be attacked, would argue a degree of apprehenfion that a good foldier fhould be afhamed of.

When a guard mounts with colours, they will make a handfome covering for the card-table at night,

L   and

and will prevent it from being stained or soiled.

When you mount the quarter-guard in camp, as soon as the men have grounded their arms, put off your sash and gorget, and immediately go to your tent, or to the grand sutler's in the rear. The serjeant can take charge of the men in your absence; and should any general officers happen to come by, you will have an opportunity to shew your activity, in running acrofs the parade to turn out the guard.

Never read the daily orders. It is beneath an officer of spirit to bestow any attention upon such nonsense; and the information you can get from them will not repay you for the trouble you are at, in decyphering them and reducing them into English. It will be sufficient to ask the serjeant, if you are for any duty.

Be

Be a conſtant attendant at the general officer's levees. If you get nothing elſe by it, you may at leaſt learn
how to ſcrape and bow, to ſimper and
to diſplay a handſome ſet of teeth, by
watching cloſely the conduct of the
aid-de-camps.

At exerciſe you muſt be continu-
ally thruſting out your ſpontoon,
ordering the men to dreſs, and
making as much noiſe as poſſible;
in order to ſhew your attention to
your duty.

When at a field day or review, you
have taken poſt in the rear for the
manual exerciſe to be performed,
you have a fine opportunity of diverting yourſelves and the ſpectators.
You ſtand very conveniently for
playing at leap-frog, or may pelt one
another with ſtones; or, if there
ſhould be ſnow on the ground, with
ſnow-balls. This will be a very

harmleſs

harmlefs relaxation, as you have nothing elfe to do, and befides the di-
verfion it will afford among your-
felves, will contribute vaftly to amufe
the foldiers and to prevent them from
puzzling their brains too much with
the bufinefs they are about.

If you are in the right wing during the firings, you muft, always
keep a pace or two in front, till you
order the men to fire; when it will
be expedient for you to ftep into the
rear, to prevent your face from being
fcorched with the powder; or you
may order two or three file on the
right of your platoon to do only the
motions of firing; which, if it dimin-
ifhes the fire of the battalion, will
at leaft fave his Majefty's ammunition.

Evening roll-calling, which drags
one from the bottle, is a moft unmilitary cuftom: for drinking is as ef-
                                    fential

fential a part of an officer's duty as fighting. Thus Alexander prided himfelf more on being able to take off half a dozen bottles at a fitting, than on all his victories over the army of Darius. If the colonel then fhould infift on the attendance of the officers, they fhould not fail to get a little mellow firft, to fhew the world that they are no milk-fops; but if any of the foldiers fhould prefume to imitate their example, they muft be confined and brought to a court-martial; for what is commendable in an officer may be in the higheft degree reprehenfible in a private man; and, as the dramatic poet obferves,

That in the captain's but a hafty word,
Which in the foldier is rank blafphemy.

When you are ordered to vifit the barracks, I would recommend it to you to confine your infpection to the outfide walls: for what can be

more

more unreasonable than to expect, that you should enter the soldiers' dirty rooms, and contaminate yourself with tasting their messes? As you are not used to eat salt pork or ammunition bread, it is impossible for you to judge whether they are good or not. Act in the same manner, when ordered to visit the hospital. It is none of your business to nurse and attend the sick. Besides, who knows but you might catch some infectious distemper? And it would be better that fifty soldiers should perish through neglect or bad treatment than that the king should lose a good officer.

Always use the most opprobrious epithets in reprimanding the soldiers, particularly men of good character: for these men it will not in the least hurt, as they will be conscious, that they do not deserve them.

When

When on leave of abſence, never come back to your time ; as that might cauſe people to think, that you had no where to ſtay, or that your friends were tired of you.

Make trenches round your marquis in camp, to carry off the water, and to prevent the ſtray-horſes from coming near enough to tread upon your tent-cords. The larger and deeper they are, the better ; that ſuch as ſtumble into them in the night may break their legs, which will be a uſeful warning to the other horſes.

If ever you have been abroad, though but to deliver drafts at Embden or Williamſtadt, give yourſelf the airs of an experienced veteran ; and in particular find fault with all parades, field days, and reviews, as of no conſequence on real ſervice. In regard to all theſe, ſay, you hate to be *playing at ſoldiers*.

CHAP.

CHAP. XII.

To the Serjeant-Major.

YOU ſhould make all the inferior non-commiſſion officers and ſoldiers call you, *Major;* and when abſent from the corps, if you are in one where the ſerjeant-major wears a laced coat and an epaulette, you may paſs yourſelf for the major of the regiment—unleſs you ſhould be aſhamed of the character. This ſame liberty may perhaps be aſſumed by the drum-major; but it is your buſineſs to prevent that rattler of parchment from taking too much upon him.

As you paſs along the front of the regiment, when telling off the diviſions from right to left, be ſure to lay your rattan pretty ſmartly upon

thoſe

thofe you name right, left or centre file; which will imprefs it to
their memory; as well as upon their
fhoulders.

In the detail for duty warn at leaft
one or two men *per* company more
than the number required, leaft any
of the latter fhould be taken ill, or
fhould come to the parade drunk or
ill dreffed; and if any of the fuper-
numeraries are your friends, or make
it worth your while, you may let
their appearance be reckoned for a
guard. What happy times were
thofe, when the adjutant and ferjeant-major have been known to
fnack five or fix fhillings a day, by
thus burning the parade!

In camp always give out the orders at fome public houfe, or booth
in the rear, at which you may oblige
the orderly ferjeants to fpend their
twopence each, for the benefit of the

M   landlord:

landlord: this in the morning will go farther towards making them drunk, than twice that ſum in the afternoon; and may therefore be at leaſt conſidered as a piece of œconomy.

When a deſerter is to be eſcorted by a party of your regiment, ſee if he does not want a ſhirt, a pair of ſhoes or ſtockings. If he does, you may venture to ſupply him with them at your own price, and charge them on the back of the route. If they are not the beſt of the kind, it is not very material; as the corporal of that, or the next party, will make the priſoner ſell or pawn them on the road; and the leſs they fetch, the leſs the party will have to expend in liquor.

C H A P.

CHAP. XIII.

To the Quarter-Master Serjeant.

YOU muſt not ſuffer the quarter-maſter to engroſs all the emoluments of office to himſelf, but muſt take care to ſecure the ſmall tithes, whilſt you leave the larger to your ſuperior. For as you ſhare, like a faithful ſquire, all the fatigues and dangers of the field, it is but reaſonable that you ſhould come in for your portion in the plunder; and, you know, diſtributive juſtice is obſerved even among thieves.

Remember this maxim; that every thing may be converted to profit. This was fully exemplified by one of your calling, who being entruſted with the delivery of candles, uſed to dip them in hot water, in order to

waſh

wash them clean; whereby he paid himself for his trouble, by sweating off a considerable quantity of the tallow, which he sold to the chandler.

Thread, cartridge paper, and ball afford variety of good perquisites, and find a ready market.

In making up blank cartridges for reviews and field-days, do not fill them too full, as they might stick in going down the barrel of the piece, and so retard the firing. Besides, too much powder might cause it to burst, and thereby kill or maim the Lord knows how many men. And it is surely much better that you should sell a little powder to the grocer, or to the boys who wish to shew their loyalty on his Majesty's birth-night, than to have it burned in waste, or perhaps to do mischief to one's friends.

As you are undertaker-general to the regiment, take particular care, when

when a foldier dies, to fee the exter-
nal offices of his funeral performed
with decency. If any young furgeon
fhould want a body for anatomical
purpofes, you may fafely anfwer it
to your confcience to furnifh him.
To be cut up and quartered is the
leaft a man can expect, who enlifts
into the army; and, after he is dead,
it is ten to one, he will know nothing of the matter. It will lighten
the burthen of the fupporters, who
have fatigue enough without that
of carrying dead bodies ; and whether you bury a corpfe or an empty
coffin, it is the fame thing to the regiment, and to the parfon—provided the latter has his fee.

In camp the rear affords your fu-
perior, the quarter-mafter, a plenti-
ful harveft; and, doubtlefs, it is but
juft, that you fhould come in for the
gleanings. Six-pence kept back from
every half-crown paid him by the
petty

petty sutlers, is surely no unreasonable deduction ; and an odd six-
pence and a dram, now and then, to
overlook irregularities, of particular
huts, are no more than you may
take without scruple.

As you are commandant of the
pioneers, you may safely let two-
thirds of them go to work for the
neighbouring farmers, and take half
their earnings. Should they be such
ungrateful dogs as to grumble or
complain, you may easily find jobs
enough for them in camp, or perhaps contrive to get them a good
flogging.

When your regiment is on the
march, and you are sent to require
the constable to press waggons, be
sure to charge for a warrant. If you
have none, it is no matter; for you
know you might have had one. And
if you should allow the waggoners
to

to reckon a mile or two more than the real diftance, or, on weighing the baggage, permit them to charge a hundred or two more than the real weight, the fhare you may get of the money will be but the juft perquifites of your office.

In loading the baggage you have an opportunity of obliging the ladies of the regiment : but remember never to let an ugly woman ride in a convenient or elevated ftation, as fhe might difgrace the corps.

When you arrive at the place the regiment refts at for the night, be fure to require more billets than you have effectives in the divifion ; and, if the conftable trufts you with them, fecure two or three of the fnuggeft houfes for yourfelf, your friend the ferjeant-major, and other particular favourites. The overplus you may convert into fhillings and half-crowns,

crowns, without any ſkill in alchymy.

Should the conſtable be ſuſpicious, and inſiſt upon ſeeing the men billeted off, tell him that you have a good many behind with the baggage, or ſick men, the time of whoſe arrival will be uncertain; and ſhould he after this perſiſt in his obſtinacy, take care that ſome of the guard knock him up twice or thrice in the dead of the night, to demand billets, as if juſt arrived. This will ſoon ſicken him; and if you do not immediately benefit by it, ſome of your ſucceeding brethren may.

In delivering out the ſmall mounting, at the annual clothing, it is very hard if you cannot get an odd ſhirt, or two or three pair of ſhoes and ſtockings. It is but robbing the colonel, who makes no ſcruple of robbing the whole regiment.

When

When in camp, you will receive
pick-axes, ſhovels, rakes, ſpades, and
other tools from the artillery. Theſe
you may let out at ſo much per
week to the labouring men in the
neighbourhood; and ſhould they be
damaged or broken, you can produce evidence, that it was done in
working.

CHAP.

CHAP. XIV.

To the Serjeant.

AS by your appointment to the halbert, you are probably at the fummit of your preferment (unlefs you have a pretty wife, fifter, or daughter) you may now begin to take a little eafe, and relax from that rigid difcipline you obferved, when corporal.

Into whatever company you are admitted, you muſt be careful to imprefs every one with an idea of your own confequence, and to make people believe, that the ferjeants are

the

the only useful and intelligent men in the corps.

You are not only to entertain a hearty contempt for your officers, but you must also take care to communicate it to the soldiers. The more you appear to despise your superiors, the greater respect, you know, your inferiors will profess for you. You will easily contrive to humbug the young subalterns, and make them do just what you please in the company : but remember, that you are to assume the merit of their good-natured actions to yourself, and to impute all the others to their own impulse.

When an officer calls you out of the ranks, run up to him with your halbert recovered, and run your fingers in his eyes, and tread upon his toes. This he will attribute to

your

your great alacrity in obeying his
orders, mixed with a modeſt confu-
ſion in addreſſing yourſelf to a man
of his importance ; and you may afterwards tell it as a good joke among
your brother ſerjeants.

Confine the ſoldiers as often as
poſſible. This will afford you an opportunity of obliging them, or their
wives, by getting them off again:
and if your officer refuſes to releaſe
them at your requeſt, you may eaſi-
ly find means to bring them off at a
court-marſhal, by ſoftening or ſup-
preſſing the evidence. Whenever
you appear againſt a ſoldier, be ſure
to give him a great character, if
called upon, in order to ſhew your
impartiality.

When you command a guard, as
ſoon as you have mounted, go to the
next alehouſe, and take poſt by the
window,

window, in order to fee that none
of the foldiers quit their guard.

When you attend a general officer
as orderly ferjeant, you muft ftick
clofe to him, wherever he goes, and
walk with your halbert charged,
the point towards the general; that
in cafe he ftops or turns fuddenly,
he may feel that you are near
him and attentive to receive his
orders.

When you are ordered to make
cartridges, moiften the paper a little. This will make them roll up
the neater, and you will get the
more credit from the quarter-mafter
for your workmanfhip. If, when
they come to be ufed, they fhould
be found unferviceable, it will be
fuppofed, that they got damage in
the quarter-mafter's ftore.

Should

Should you be reprimanded by your officers for being intoxicated, and having neglected your duty, tell them, that some serjeants of other regiments, old acquaintances of yours, with whom you had formerly served, had come to pay you a visit, and that you were obliged to entertain them, as they do their brother officers, for the honour of the corps.

Whenever you mount guard in garrison or quarters, be sure to leave it upon record on the wainscotting or ceiling of the guard-room. This practice, besides the ornament it will afford the room, will form a series of useful and authentic historical tables for the regiments that succeed you.

If you have a knack at recruiting, and can get sent on that service with

an

an extravagant young fubaltern, your
fortune is made ; that is, if you
mind what you are about ; as the
more he runs out, the more you
ought to get. You may quiet your
confcience, fhould it be troublefome,
by confidering, that if you did not
fleece him, fome one elfe would, and
that the money fo acquired is better
in your pocket, than in thofe of a
pack of whores and gamblers. Nor
need you fear any thing from his
future refentment in cafe of a dif-
covery ; as it is ten to one but the
confequences of fix months recruiting will oblige him to fell out, and
quit the regiment for ever.

Whenever you beat up in a country town, though your officer fhould
be the youngeft enfign in the army
and the fon of a valet de chambre,
you muft not fail to dub him captain, and ftile him his honour at
every

every word. You may alfo give it out, that he is heir to a very large eftate in fome county between Cornwall and Berwick, but you forget the name. This will give him importance, and, what is more material, credit; and as to the untruth, it is at worft a white lie; and, befides, if detraction is a vice, its oppofite muft be a virtue.

In enlifting men never mind whether they are fit for the fervice or not. If they cannot ferve, they are the more likely to pay the fmart.

But remember, that you are to furnifh at leaft one, if not two or more young recruits, for every man you inlift. This will be doing a benefit to the parifh: for you give them in lieu of the recruit you trepan one much younger, who confequently muft be of

more

more value, as his country will enjoy
the advantage of his ſervices the
longer.

In any diſpute reſpecting the inliſt-
ing of a man, you may ſafely give
your teſtimony or oath for the fairneſs
of the tranſaction, although you were
not preſent, nor ſaw any thing of the
matter. It is for the good of the
ſervice.

As ſoon as a recruit has ſpent all his
bounty money, which with your kind
aſſiſtance, and that of the drummer
and party, he may do in a very ſhort
time, endeavour to put him out of
conceit with the ſervice, that he may
attempt to deſert. This, if he is an
innocent country fellow, he will manage in ſo awkward a manner, as to
enable you to retake him immediately.
Here is at once twenty ſhillings dead,
over and above the regimental reward ;
and it will beſides procure you the

O   cha-

character of a vigilant and alert officer.
Should he however escape, bring in a
long account against him for necessaries and money advanced, though you
never furnished him with a single article, or lent him a farthing. This you
may safely do, as he will not be present
to contradict you, and should he be
afterwards taken, the word of a deserter, guilty of perjury, cannot be put
in competition with your accounts.

If on service you detect a soldier
marauding, be sure to seize upon the
plunder, whether pig, lamb, goose,
or other poultry; but as it may be the
first offence, and a reprimand may deter him from the like practices in future, you need not report him to the
commanding officer; and if you eat
the stolen goods, it is only to prevent
the sin of waste.

When you have the rear-guard in
camp, you may take up your station
at

at one of the huts, and leave the guard
to the corporal. It is no more than
what is done by the officer of the
quarter-guard ; and if the rounds
fhould by accident fall upon your
guard, whilft you are miffing, fay,
that you were juft gone to vifit your
fentinels, or to quell a riot.

In order to turn the penny, contrive,
when in camp, to let your wife keep
a hut in the rear, and fell ale and gin.
The ftanding orders only fay, *you* fhall
not do it, but do not prohibit *her*.
Here you may fettle with your men ;
and if they fpend the greateft part of
their pay in liquor, it is no more than
they would do elfewhere, and you may
as well have their money as another.

C H A P.

CHAP. XV.

To the Corporal.

AS you are but one ftep below the
ferjeant, and often have the honour of reprefenting him, as launce-
ferjeant, you may juftly avail yourfelf
of many articles of the advice to that
officer.   Some few particulars are folely
applicable to your appointment: rela-
tive to thefe I fhall give you a hint or
two.

It is your office to poft the fentinels,
and to fee that they are properly relieved; and a difagreeable office it is
in a dark, cold, and ftormy night.
You may therefore in bad weather fave
yourfelf that trouble, and fend the relief by themfelves.   This will be a
means of teaching them how to perform their duty, when corporals; and
surely

furely they muft be very unfit for fentinels, if they cannot be trufted alone.

When commanding an efcort with
a deferter, I need not tell you, that
his fhirt, fhoes, and ftockings will produce a pot or two of beer, or a glafs
of gin. The prifoner is fure to get
supplied, when he comes to the regiment, and it is but one flogging for
all. Perfuade him likewife to pretend
lamenefs; you may then charge double
for carriage by a cart, horfe, or return
chaife, and drink the produce; befides faving your labour and fhoes.

When you efcort a man to the field
for punifhment, you may let him drink
as much liquor as he can procure. This
will in fome meafure deaden the pain,
and prevent him from difgracing himfelf and the regiment, by becoming
what the drummers term a nightin-
gale.

On

On the rear guard, when the ſer-
jeant has left you (which he will infal-
libly do, ſoon after he has mounted)
you become commanding officer, and
have an opportunity of obliging the
ſoldiers. Permit, therefore, at leaſt
one-half of them to go about their buſineſs till it is their turn to ſtand ſen-
tinel; and, ſhould they be miſſed, ſay
that they are juſt gone into the rear,
or that one of them was taken in a fit,
and that the reſt are gone with him to
his tent, or to the ſurgeon.

Make it a general rule to prevent all
diſorders and crimes from coming to
the ears of the officers, as it would only
vex them, and make them uneaſy.
Beſides, the contrary would procure
you the hateful title of a tell-tale or
informer.

Teach the young recruits the proper
uſe of their arms, when off duty—as,
to make a horſe to hang their wet
cloaths

cloaths upon with the firelocks—with the bayonet to carry their ammunition loaves, toaſt cheeſe and pork, and ſtir the fire: it might otherwiſe contract ruſt for want of uſe.

In order to get the character of a ſmart fellow at exerciſe, looſen the pins on the ſtock of your firelock, to make the motions tell. If the piece get damage by it, it is no great matter; your captain, you know, pays the piper; and it is right that he ſhould pay to hear ſuch martial muſic.

As it is the buſineſs of a good non-commiſſion-officer to be active in taking up all deſerters, when, on the march, or at any other time, you obſerve any ducks, geeſe, or fowls, that have eſcaped the bounds of their confinement, immediately apprehend them, and take them along with you, that they may be tried for their offence at a proper ſeaſon. This will prevent the ſoldiers from marauding.

When

When the regiment attends divine service, should you be ordered to stay without to keep the soldiers to their devotions, see if there is not an alehouse near at hand, that commands a view of the church door, whence you may most conveniently watch their motions.

Yours is a troublesome and fatiguing office. You must, however, bustle through as well as you can, doing your duty, when you cannot help it; and keeping up your spirits with good geneva, when it is to be had, and with the hopes of arriving at the ease and dignity of the halbert.

C H A P.

CHAP. XVI.

To the Drum-Major.

YOU are firſt painter to the regiment, and your principal duty is, to inſtruct the young academicians in the art. Your pencils indeed are none of the ſofteſt; and though you do not aim at the grace of *Raphael*, or the grandeur of *Michael Angelo*, yet you muſt not yield to *Titian* in colouring.

You are alſo the *Paris*, if not the *Adonis* of the regiment; and every judge of diſcipline will eſtimate the goodneſs of the corps by the taſte and ſplendour of your trappings.

The title of Major is as applicable to you, as to the Serjeant-major. You ſhould therefore inſiſt on that appellation from all your drummers; and as

P you

you are, in all probability, the hand-
fomeſt, the fineſt and the youngeſt
fellow of the two, you will be the
moſt likely to paſs for the major of
the regiment.

It being your office to furniſh the
pencils for the young painters, vulgar-
ly called cat-o'-nine-tails, and as you
are paid by the delinquents for the uſe
of them; you may, in imitation of
other contractors, put them off with
ſecond-hand ones, which by a little
waſhing will be as clean as ever, and
will be much ſofter to the back. If
this is not diſcovered by the adjutant,
or he is good-natured enough to wink
at it, no harm is done; your cuſtomers
will have no reaſon to complain: beſides, if they do, it is no more than
you are to expect; for do what you
will, one may venture to affirm, you
never ſend any of them away well
pleaſed. Indeed this contract for whip-
cord might be made a very beneficial
one,

one, was it not for that unfeeling dog, the adjutant : as you could, if left to yourfelf, accommodate a cuftomer, according to any price he is willing to give, from the ftiffeft cord to the half-twifted packthread.

At a punifhment, do not fail to exercife your rattan on your drummers, whether they favour the delinquent or not. It will keep them up to their duty ; and every one knows it is better to prevent an offence, than to punifh it : befides, it may fave your own fhoulders from being rubbed over by the adjutant's towel.

As you are poft-mafter-general to the regiment, much is to be gained from that department ; and that by the fimpleft means—only by charging the officers and men for letters they never had, and double poftage for what they really receive. With refpect to many of the officers, fuch as the command-

ing

ing officer, adjutant, quarter-master,
&c. you may safely do it, as the money does not come out of their own
pockets, but is charged in the contin-
gent bill. They will not, therefore,
give themselves much trouble about
the matter; and, as to the private
men, you, as a non-commission officer,
may easily brow-beat them, should
they question your accounts; and, in
matter of conscience, as you are often
obliged to trust a long time for the
payment of their postage, it is barely
getting a little more than common interest for your money.

Besides the appointments already
mentioned, you are also officially keeper
of the *menagerie* to the corps. If the
colonel, or any other officer, has a large
wolf, or bull-dog, or the regiment
any tame animal that follows it, such
as an ape, a bear, a fawn, or a goat,
they will assuredly be placed under
your care. This will be a regular
income

income to you; and you may occasionally bring in a bill for depredations which they never committed.

In winter-quarters, or at any time when you have nothing else to do, flog all your drummers round. If they do not then deserve it, it is pretty certain they lately have, or shortly will: besides, correction tends to keep them good, when they are so.

If you should hear of any person being dangerously ill in any town or garrison, when you beat through the streets, take care to brace your drums well, and to make a confounded noise, as you pass under their windows. This may sometimes procure you a perquifite.

In marching by the commanding officer, when you beat the short troop, look as stern as possible, and appear as if you could eat him up at a mouthful.
When

When you pitch on a place for practice in garrifon, let it be as near the town as poffible, that the officers may conftantly hear the boys at *daddy-mammy*, and be thereby convinced that you do not fuffer them to be idle. If it is clofe to an hofpital, a public fchool, or a church, it will be fo much the better ; as the found of the drums will amufe the fick, divert the boys, and keep the old women awake at their devotions.

C H A P.

CHAP. XVII.

To the Drummer.

BY your profeſſion you are evidently deſtined to make a noiſe in the world: and your party-coloured coat and drum-carriage, like the zone of *Venus*, or halter about the neck of a felon, makes you appear a pretty fellow in the eyes of the ladies. So that you may always, if not over-modeſt, (which I muſt own is not often the failing of gentlemen of your calling) be ſure of bringing off a girl from every quarter. After infecting her with a certain diſeaſe, and ſelling her clothes, you may introduce her to the officers, your employments making you a dependent on *Mercury* as well as *Apollo*. This will at leaſt inſure you the thanks of the ſurgeon and his mate.

As

As it is neceſſary that a ſoldier ſhould know all the uſes of his arms, permit me to obſerve to you, that a drum and its appurtenances may, in the hands of a clever fellow, anſwer many good purpoſes beſides that of being beaten on. Should a flock of geeſe or ducks obſtruct your line of march, two or three may be ſafely and ſecretly lodged in it ; and the drum caſe will hold peas, beans, apples and potatoes, when the havreſack is full.

Whenever you fall in with a horſeman on the road, you may try the rider's ſkill, and the horſe's mettle, by beating the grenadier's march juſt under his noſe. Should the rider be diſmounted, and get his arm broken, or his ſkull fractured, it is no more than he deſerves, for not paying a due reſpect to your cloth, in taking himſelf out of the road ; and, after all, it is not your fault, but the horſe's.

When

When you mount guard with an officer, put by half the allowance of coals. This is your undoubted perquifite, by ufage for time immemorial; and the Quarter-mafter-ferjeant will help you to a chap to take them off your hands; or, at worft, you may exchange them at the cantine for liquor.

Never fweep the guard-room till the guard is juft going to be relieved: the unfettled duft will prove to the relieving officer, that you have not omitted that part of your duty.

All bottles, glaffes, &c. brought with the officers' dinner, and left by miftake, are, as well as the remains of the provifion, your property: and fhould a ftray filver fpoon happen to be amongft them, you may venture to take it into your protection, left it fhould fall into difhoneft hands.

Q

When

When ordered to put the ſentence of a Court-martial into execution, you will do it according to your opinion of the matter; and, if the priſoner ſhould, whilſt in cuſtody, have treated you to a pot of beer, or to a dram, you know how to be grateful.

Should you arrive to ſuch a degree of excellence, as to be appointed an orderly drummer, you may paſs your time very comfortably; particularly, if you have an old, and not very ſkilful major, as he will want your aſſiſtance to put the regiment through its exerciſe. But, in that caſe, don't fail to conſider your own importance, and to take upon you accordingly: you may then bid defiance to the drum-major and the adjutant.

You muſt inform yourſelf of the meaning of the different beats of the drum; and endeavour to conform to the

the original intention of them. Thus,
reveiller fignifies to wake. Therefore,
in performing this part of your duty
in garrifon, you muft continue beating,
not only till you have awakened the
fentinels, and the officer of the guard,
but alfo till you have roufed all the
neighbouring inhabitants.

When parading before the head-
quarters to beat off the troop, re-
treat, or tattoo, contrive, by bracing,
tapping and trying your drum, to
make as much noife as poffible.
This will ferve to convince the commanding officer of your punctuality.

CHAP.

CHAPTER XVIII.

To the Private Soldier.

AS a private foldier, you fhould
confider all your officers as your
natural enemies, with whom you are
in a perpetual ftate of warfare: you
fhould reflect that they are conftantly
endeavouring to withhold from you all
your juft dues, and to impofe on you
every unneceffary hardfhip; and this
for the mere fatisfaction of doing you
an injury. In your turn, therefore,
make it a point to deceive and defraud
them, every poffible opportunity; and
more particularly the officers of the
company to which you belong.

Firft then, take every method of
getting into your captain's debt; and,
when you are pretty handfomely on
his books, turn out a volunteer for
foreign

foreign service, or else desert; and after waiting for a proclamation, or an act of grace, surrender yourself to some other corps.

On duty, as soon as the corporal has posted you sentry, and left you, (if he has given himself the trouble of coming out with the relief) endeavour to accommodate yourself as conveniently as you can, the health of every good soldier being of the utmost consequence to the service. For this purpose, if you have a sentry-box, get some stones, and make yourself a seat; or bore two large holes in the opposite sides, through which you may pass your stick, or for want of it, your firelock. Thus seated, in order that you may not fall asleep, which would be rather improper and dangerous for a sentry, sing or whistle some merry tune, as loud as possible: this will both keep you awake, and convince people that you really are so.

In

In camp, where you cannot have the benefit of a box, as foon as you are pofted, carefully ground your arms in fome dry place, a good foldier being always careful of his arms ; and, wrapping yourfelf up in your watch-coat, fit or lie down in the lee of fome officer's marquis ; and, to pafs the tedious hours away, whiftle or fing, as before directed ; and if ever you fmoke, there cannot be a better time to take a pipe.

If you are fentinel at the tent of one of the field-officers, you need not challenge in the fore part of the evening, for fear of difturbing his honour, who perhaps may be reading, writing, or entertaining company. But as foon as he is gone to bed, roar out every ten minutes at leaft, *Who comes there?* though nobody is paffing. This will give him a favourable idea of your alertnefs ; and though his flumbers may be broken, yet will they be the

more

more pleafing, when he finds that he repofes in perfect fecurity. When the hour of relief approaches, keep conftantly crying out, *Relief, relief!* it will prevent the guard from forgetting you, and prove that you are not afleep.

Perhaps it may be unneceffary to inform you, that in relieving you may go without your arms, and take the firelock from the man you relieve. By this contrivance none of the firelocks, but thofe of the fentries, will be wet, or out of order.

On a march, fhould you be one of the baggage guard, put your arms, knapfack, and havrefack on the waggon; and if they are loft, or your firelock broken, make out fome ftory to your captain, who at all events muft replace and repair them.

Should

Should you, by accident, have pawned or fold your neceffaries, feign ficknefs on the day they are reviewed, and borrow thofe of any foldier, whofe company is not infpected. You may, in your turn, oblige him in the like manner; and, if this cannot be done, contrive to get confined for fome trivial neglect, till the review is over.

If your comrade deferts, you may fafely fell your whole kit, and charge him with having ftolen it: fhould he be caught, and deny it, nobody will believe him.

If the duty runs hard, you may eafily fham fick, by fwallowing a quid of tobacco. Knock your elbow againft the wall, or your tent-pole, and it will accelerate the circulation to the quicknefs of a fever. Quick lime and foap will give you a pair of fore legs, that would deceive the furgeon-general himfelf: and the rheumatifm

is

is an admirable pretence, not eafily difcovered. If you fhould be fent to an hofpital in London, contrive to draw money from the agent; it is your officer's bufinefs to look to the payment.

When you are really taken ill, flap your hat, let your hair hang down loofe upon your fhoulders, wear a dirty handkerchief about your neck, unhook your fkirts, and ungaiter your ftockings. Thefe are all privileges of ficknefs.

If your mefs have changed their marketing for gin, or any other good liquor, and have nothing to put into the pot, carefully wrap up a puppy or a brickbat in a cloth, and call it a fheep's head, or a pudding. This you may very fafely do, as it is an hundred to one that your officer will not be at the pains to examine it.

R   At

At a field-day, ſtop up the touch-hole of your piece with cobbler's wax, or ſome other ſubſtance. This will prevent your firing, and ſave you the trouble of cleaning your arms : beſides, unleſs the quarter-maſter-ſerjeant and his pioneers are uncommonly careful, you may ſecrete ſome cartridges to ſell to the boys of the town to make ſquibs.

In the firings always be ſure to fill your pan as full of powder as poſſible ; it will cauſe much fun in the ranks, by burning your right-hand man : and on the right wing it will alſo burn the officers ; who, perhaps, to ſave their pretty faces, may order the right-hand file of each platoon not to fire, and thus ſave them the trouble of diſmounting their firelocks, and waſhing the barrel, after the exerciſe is over.

In coming down as front rank, be ſure to do it briſkly, and let the toe

of

of the butt firſt touch the ground.
By this you may poſſibly break the
ſtock ; which will ſave you the trouble of further exerciſe that day : and
your captain will be obliged to make
good the damage. The ſame effect
may be produced by coming from the
ſhoulder to the order, at two motions,
eſpecially on the pavement in a garriſon town.

As firing ball may be attended with
accidents, and beſides gives a ſoldier
the unneceſſary trouble of cleaning his
piece, when you load with cartridge,
put the ball downwards ; which will
ſettle the matter for that day.

When you want to ſkrew in a freſh
flint, do it with your bayonet : if this
notches it, it will be uſeful as a ſaw,
and you will beſides ſhew your inge-
nuity in making it ſerve for purpoſes
for which it never was intended :
though, indeed, this weapon may
be

be faid to be the moft handy of any a foldier carries. It is an excellent inftrument for digging potatoes, onions, or turnips. Stuck in the ground, it makes a good candleftick; and it will on occafion ferve either to kill a mudlark, or to keep an impertinent boor at a proper diftance, whilft your comrades are gathering his apples.

Should you get to be an officer's fervant, you may immediately commence fine gentleman. If he is about your own fize, you may wear his fhirts and ftockings; and fhould you tear them in putting them on, it is his fault for having them made fo fmall.

When he is on guard, you may invite company to his marquis, and it is hard if you cannot get a key that will open his canteens.

If on the march he gives you a canteen with a lock to carry, this is truly

muzzling

muzzling the ox; which is forbidden
in fcripture. You may therefore punifh him, by breaking the bottle, and
drinking his liquor: there will be no
difficulty to bring witneffes to prove
that it was done by a fall.

When you wait on him at the mefs,
you may eafily contrive to pocket half
a fowl, a duck, a tongue, or fome
fuch convenient morfel; and you and
your brethren muft be very awkward
and improvident, if you can't filch
fome beer, or a bottle of wine, to
drink with it. Some futlers are kind
enough to poor fervants to fcore a pot
or two of ale for their benefit.

If you are bât-man to an officer,
your perquifites are certain. Sell half
the forage to the futlers, who keep
horfes or affes: if they don't pay you
in money, they will in gin. As a
chriftian is more worthy than a beaft,
it is better your mafter's horfes fhould
want than you.

When

When in quarters, fhould your landlord be uncivil, there are various methods by which you may bring him to reafon. If he refufes to fub-fift you at the rated allowance, you may foon force him to it, by roafting a cat, a dog, or an old boot, at the landlord's fire: for it is no bufinefs of his, what you drefs for your own dinner.

You may be fure that, go into what quarters you will, the landlord will heartily wifh you out of them. You fhould therefore make it a point to give him good caufe for it; as it is hard a man fhould be hated and def-pifed without reafon.

Qui capit, ille facit.

F I N I S.

INSTRUCTION

Instruction united with Amusement.

THE following SELECTIONS form confeſſedly the moſt entertaining and intereſting collection, for youth of both ſexes, in the Engliſh language; and are all printed uniform in ten Pocket Volumes; each of which may be had ſingly for half a crown, or the whole for one pound five ſhillings.

They form a handſome and uſeful preſent.

As that great luminary Dr. Johnson ſtrongly re-commends, in the fourth volume of his Rambler, ſelect-ing the BEST thoughts of our BEST writers, it is rather ſingular that this truly reſpectable Author'a advice has not been adopted before.

The Volumes now Publiſhed, are

The BEAUTIES of

SHAKSPEARE,	GOLDSMITH,
MILTON,	SWIFT,
THOMSON,	STERNE,
YOUNG,	WATTS,
POPE,	AND
JOHNSON,	FIELDING.

With the Lives of each Author, and their HEADS neatly engraved by TROTTER.

The Beauties of MILTON, THOMSON, and YOUNG, are all contained in one Volume.

Every looſe and indelicate expreſſion is carefully omitted in SWIFT and STERNE.

The

The Monthly Review, in speaking of the Beauties of JOHNSON, says, "We heartily wish this selection "success among Youth, for whose improvement, par- "ticularly in schools, it seems principally intended."

Though the whole collection has been published but a short period, most of them have gone through several editions, and been introduced into the principal schools in and about London.

Printed for George Kearsley, at No. 46, in Fleet-street.

*** As these BEAUTIES are so generally read at home, there can be no doubt but they will be as well received abroad; particularly in the East and West-Indies. Those who buy them for exportation, will have a proper allowance.